Original title:
From Heartbreak

Copyright © 2024 Swan Charm
All rights reserved.

Author: Linda Leevike
ISBN HARDBACK: 978-9916-89-679-2
ISBN PAPERBACK: 978-9916-89-680-8
ISBN EBOOK: 978-9916-89-681-5

Whispers in the Sanctuary

In quiet halls where echoes dwell,
The sacred words begin to swell.
Heartbeats mingle, spirits rise,
In whispered prayers, we touch the skies.

Beneath the arch, with hands outspread,
We seek the light, we seek the bread.
Each sigh a note of love and grace,
In stillness found, we find our place.

The candles flicker, shadows play,
A gentle guide to lead our way.
In gratitude, our voices blend,
In the sanctuary, hearts transcend.

With every breath, a promise made,
In sacred trust, we are remade.
Together strong, we face the night,
With faith our lantern, shining bright.

The Pilgrimage of Pain

Along the path where shadows creep,
We walk in silence, our souls in deep.
Each step a burden, heavy, worn,
Yet through the struggle, strength is born.

The road is long, the sky is gray,
In pain we find a brighter day.
With every tear, a lesson learned,
In fire forged, our hearts now burned.

The mountains rise, the valleys low,
Yet in the journey, love will grow.
We gather hope in every sigh,
In trials faced, we learn to fly.

So let the storms around us rage,
In faith we turn a healing page.
The pilgrimage, though fraught with strife,
Brings forth the beauty of our life.

Redemption in Shadows

In shadows cast by weary days,
A flicker glows in hidden ways.
Through darkest nights, a whisper calls,
In stillness found, redemption sprawls.

We search for light in depths of grace,
Each stumble leads us to embrace.
The grace that mends the broken glass,
In every flaw, our spirits pass.

The past may haunt, but hope will rise,
From ashes cold, our spirits fly.
In every shadow, love is sown,
Redemption sings, we are not alone.

Embrace the light that breaks the dawn,
With every breath, new life is drawn.
Together we shall stand and fight,
For in the shadows, shines the light.

Lost Sheep, Wandering Soul

A wanderer beneath the sun,
In search of peace, my heart undone.
The trails I roam, a path unknown,
I seek the place I can call home.

In fields of green, and skies of blue,
I hear the call, a voice so true.
It beckons gently, soft and clear,
In every heartbeat, love draws near.

Though lost at times, hope lights the way,
With footsteps guided, come what may.
The Shepherd calls; I hear the sound,
In aching hearts, grace can be found.

No longer lost, in stillness found,
With faith restored, I stand my ground.
For every soul that looks for peace,
In love we find our sweet release.

Prayers Among the Ruins

In shadows cast by stones so cold,
Soft whispers rise, in faith we hold.
Amidst the wreckage, souls seek light,
Their hearts a beacon, burning bright.

Each prayer a thread, a fragile bond,
In silent hopes, of mercy fond.
To lift our eyes beyond the pain,
And find His grace in every rain.

The ruins speak of battles fought,
In every crack, is wisdom sought.
With humbled hearts, we answer call,
For even lost, His love is all.

We gather here, a faithful throng,
With heavy hearts, yet voices strong.
Each tear a sign of healing grace,
We rise again, we seek His face.

In prayers among the crumbling walls,
We hear the echo of He who calls.
Through trials faced, our spirits soar,
In ruins, love endures evermore.

The Veil of Wounded Love

Behind the veil of hearts so torn,
A sacred ache from love, reborn.
Through trials deep, the soul takes wing,
In wounds, the hope of healing sings.

Each scar a testament to fate,
A loving touch that conquers hate.
Though pains may linger, tides will turn,
In every loss, a lesson learned.

We seek the light in darkest night,
For in our sorrow shines His might.
With every breath, we mend the thread,
Of dreams once lost but not quite dead.

In gentle whispers, love remains,
Bringing solace through our pains.
With open arms, we trust the way,
To find our peace with each new day.

The veil may cloak, yet holds no fear,
For love transcends, it draws us near.
In wounded hearts, divine embrace,
Through trials faced, we find our grace.

Incense of Regret

The scent of time, a bitter balm,
In shadows deep, it weaves a psalm.
Each memory a trail of smoke,
In silence felt, the heart awoke.

We gather remnants of the past,
Embers that glow, yet seldom last.
In every sigh, a prayer ascends,
For broken paths that love transcends.

With incense rising, we confess,
Our hearts entwined in loneliness.
Sorrow wraps around our soul,
In every flicker, we seek whole.

Yet from despair, a hope ignites,
As spirits soar to reach the heights.
Regret may linger, teach us well,
In lessons learned, we find the bell.

In fragrant dusk, we raise our hands,
To seek forgiveness, love expands.
With every breath, a chance to mend,
For through regret, our hearts can transcend.

The Covenant of Forgotten Promises

In whispers of a time once known,
A covenant etched, yet overgrown.
With every vow, we drew a line,
In sacred trust, our souls entwined.

Yet storms of life have forged a path,
That dims the glow of loving math.
Forgotten words like shadows lay,
Yet hope remains to guide the way.

We seek to lift the veil of time,
In earnest hearts, we seek to climb.
With faith as anchor, love as guide,
A promise waits, no need to hide.

The past may echo, loud and stark,
Yet in our hearts, ignites a spark.
For every promise made in pain,
Can bloom anew like flowers rain.

In the covenant of love so true,
We find our way, me and you.
Though memories fade, the bond remains,
In every heart, our love sustains.

Hope in the Desert of Regret

In the expanse, barren and wide,
Hope blooms softly, a heart's hidden guide.
Through shadows of sorrow, it seeks the light,
Whispers of grace unveil the night.

Every step is a prayer on the sand,
Faith like an oasis, a gentle hand.
Memories linger, yet courage remains,
The soul, like a phoenix, breaks its chains.

With each tear, a seed of belief,
From despair's depths, springs joy, sweet relief.
The past may haunt with its bitter taste,
But in the void, love's truth is embraced.

Gentle winds carry the cries of old,
Turning to stories of courage bold.
In the desert's heart, a promise stands,
Hope transcends trials through divine hands.

Revelations in the Quiet

In the stillness, the spirit awakes,
Whispers of truth in the silence break.
Clarity dances in soft, golden rays,
Moments of wonder, lost in the maze.

Each breath is a blessing, a sacred chant,
In solitude found, the heart's soft lament.
Visions unfold in the gentle embrace,
The soul drinks deep from the well of grace.

Time stretches thin like a thread of light,
Illuminating paths in the deepest night.
Each secret revealed brings wisdom anew,
In the quiet, the world's fabric grew.

Listen closely, for love's refrain,
In the silence, there's joy and pain.
Revelations whisper, soft as a prayer,
In the calm, the heart learns to care.

Silent Confessions of the Damned

In the shadows, where lost souls weep,
Silent confessions buried deep.
Each echo a sigh in the chilling dark,
Yearning for light, igniting a spark.

Chains of remorse, heavy they cling,
The weight of the past, an unyielding sting.
Yet hope lingers in the deepest abyss,
A flicker of warmth, a gentle kiss.

Beneath the ruins, a heart beats strong,
Finding redemption where it feels wrong.
Every tear shed softens the stone,
Amidst the ashes, grace is sown.

Forgiveness blooms in the hardest places,
Shattering silence with tender embraces.
The damned shall rise from sorrow's hold,
In the quiet, redemption unfolds.

The Canticle of Forgotten Affection

In the twilight, where shadows blend,
Sing the songs of love that transcend.
Whispers of joy, once vibrant and bright,
Now echo through the stillness of night.

Each memory dances, a flickering flame,
Calling to hearts, yet leaving no name.
Though time may fade what was once divine,
In the soul's quiet, affection will shine.

The stars above recall every laugh,
Writing their tales in the universe's half.
Through seasons of loss, hope does remain,
A canticle sweet, in joy and in pain.

Let love be your anchor, let it be your song,
In the depths of the night, where you still belong.
For affection lingers, though time drifts away,
In the heart, ever vibrant, it holds its sway.

Labyrinths of Loss

In shadows deep where sorrows lie,
A path emerges, but none know why.
Each twist and turn, a silent plea,
A search for hope, to set us free.

We wander through the endless maze,
In memories lost, our hearts ablaze.
Whispers echo of love once near,
Yet in the void, we find our fear.

Yet faith a torch in darkest night,
Guiding souls toward aching light.
As we traverse this heartfelt quest,
We find our peace, our weary rest.

Through the tears and trials we face,
In every loss, His truth we trace.
In labyrinths of grief we trove,
Awakening the light of love.

For in our wounds, a seed must grow,
Faith's tender grace will surely sow.
From loss we'll bloom, like flowers bright,
In darkness, we will find our light.

Sanctuary of the Unseen

Amidst the stillness, whispers dwell,
In sacred halls where shadows fell.
The heart may ache, yet here we stand,
In unseen grace, a gentle hand.

Each prayer we lift, a soft embrace,
In quietude, we find His face.
A sanctuary of hope and trust,
In faith, we rise from ashes, dust.

Voices echo like softest chime,
In every moment, transcending time.
The unseen path, a sacred thread,
We weave our dreams where angels tread.

In trials faced and burdens borne,
Divine protection each day reborn.
The sanctuary holds us tight,
In every dark, reveals the light.

So gather close, all weary hearts,
In silent love, the journey starts.
In unseen realms, we stand as one,
Embracing grace till day is done.

Epiphany Amidst the Ruins

In broken walls where silence grows,
A spark ignites, and truth bestows.
Amidst the ruins, life breaks free,
An epiphany for all to see.

The past may tarnish, but can't confine,
For in despair, His light will shine.
From ashes rise a sacred flame,
Transforming loss, we find His name.

With every step through shadows cast,
A journey shines, the die is cast.
In broken pieces, beauty found,
In gentle whispers, love unbound.

So let us walk this hallowed ground,
In hope renewed, our hearts unbound.
For every ruin tells a tale,
An epiphany, we shall unveil.

From crumbling faith, a vision clear,
In every loss, we persevere.
To rise again with courage bold,
In shattered dreams, new life unfolds.

The Covenant of Lost Time

In sacred bonds of time's embrace,
We gather lost, yet find our place.
Each moment passes, gentle sigh,
Yet in the depths, our spirits fly.

The covenant we weave with tears,
Through trials faced throughout the years.
In every loss, a lesson learned,
For wisdom gained is light affirmed.

In whispers soft, time speaks to all,
In every rise, we will not fall.
The past may haunt, but joy will bloom,
In every corner of the room.

For every shadow holds a choice,
In silence, we hear the still, small voice.
The covenant binds our hearts so tight,
In every loss, we find the light.

So let us cherish moments fleet,
In every heartbeat, love's heartbeat.
Together we forge our sacred chime,
In unity's grace, the lost finds time.

In the Name of What Was

In the silence of ancient halls,
We gather whispers of the past.
In the name of what was sacred,
From echoes, our shadows are cast.

Golden chalices raise to the sky,
In a prayer for the days that remain.
With reverence, we ask the Divine,
To guide us through joy and through pain.

In the heart of each fading flame,
Lies the story of lives once lived.
In the name of what was revered,
We seek solace, and grace is given.

Beneath the stars, we tread softly,
Each heartbeat sings of the night.
In the name of what found us here,
We surrender to the sacred light.

With each dawn, we arise anew,
Finding hope in the threads of the past.
In the name of what was, we bind,
To the truths that will forever last.

Martyrs of Memory

In the vale where shadows dwell,
Martyrs rise with silent grace.
They whisper tales in hushed tones,
In the dark, they find their place.

With broken hearts and weary souls,
They carry burdens of our plight.
In the forgotten, strength endures,
Guiding us through the lost night.

Each tear shed is a sacred vow,
A testament of battles fought.
In the warmth of gathered souls,
We remember, lessons taught.

Their echoes live in every heart,
A chorus of love undying.
In the silence where truth resides,
Martyrs' spirits keep on flying.

Through sacrifice, their spirits soar,
In memory, they find their voice.
Martyrs of time, we stand in awe,
In remembrance, we rejoice.

Inner Sanctum of Solitude

In the quietude of my heart's core,
I find solace, peace, and more.
Within the walls of sacred thought,
Joys and battles through silence fought.

Here, I seek the stillness profound,
Echoes of grace, where love is found.
The whispers of truth softly call,
In solitude, I rise, I fall.

With every breath, the spirit sings,
In the depth, the soul takes wings.
Through shadows cast by heavy pain,
The light of hope begins to reign.

In the sanctuary of the mind,
There lies a treasure few can find.
Amidst the chaos of the day,
Inner peace shall lead the way.

In this retreat from worldly haste,
I embrace the moment, love laid bare.
In solitude, my spirit thrives,
In the sacred, true light arrives.

The Testament of Letting Go

In the soft dawn, I lay my weight,
Releasing burdens, uniting fate.
In the grip of the heart's still night,
I blend shadows into the light.

With open hands, I set them free,
The chains of sorrow, once part of me.
Each moment cherished, now must fade,
In faith, I walk unafraid.

The memories drift like autumn leaves,
Teaching me how to believe.
In the silence, I feel the grace,
Of letting go, a warm embrace.

With every tear, a lesson learned,
In the fire of pain, my heart has turned.
Through the ashes, I rise anew,
With hope and love guiding me through.

So here I stand, in truth and peace,
The testament of my soul's release.
In faith, I find my way to grow,
A sacred path, the art of letting go.

Asceticism in the Shadows

In silent woods, the night conceals,
A heart that yearns, yet never feels.
Beneath the stars, the whispers sigh,
Of truth that hides, where none deny.

A life of lack, a path so grim,
Yet in the dark, the soul grows dim.
For every gain, a loss must weave,
Ascetic dreams, we dare to believe.

In shadows cast, a light shall break,
The world may fade, but hearts awake.
Through sacrifice, the spirit soars,
In humble peace, our spirit roars.

The void of want, where love is found,
In simple things, our grace unbound.
With every step, the night will yield,
The soul's true strength, in silence healed.

Divine Silence after the Storm

The thunder fades, the winds retreat,
In quiet grace, the heart shall meet.
A gentle peace, like balm, descends,
Where faith endures, the spirit bends.

Each raindrop falls like tears of prayer,
In sacred stillness, we lay bare.
A moment found in loss and gain,
In silence sweet, we bear our pain.

From chaos born, a quiet soul,
In every breath, we find our whole.
The storm may rage, yet love remains,
In whispered tones, the heart restrains.

A tranquil heart, like ancient lore,
In silence, find the truth we bore.
In every trial, a chance to rise,
To hear the voice beyond the skies.

Purgatory of Patchwork Hearts

Stitched together with threads of grace,
A tapestry of every face.
In shadows deep, the heart's lament,
Each piece a story, soul's imprint.

As fragments fall, we stand as one,
In love's embrace, the battle won.
Through pain and joy, we weave our fate,
In purgatory, we contemplate.

With every stitch, new love is born,
In broken ties, the heart's adorn.
Through trials fierce, we grow and mend,
In every heart, a faithful friend.

Embrace the flaws, the beauty shows,
In perfect gaps, a love that grows.
The patchwork taught, in pain we trust,
In sacred bonds, our love is just.

The Lost Sheep of Love

In fields afar, a lone one strays,
Through valleys cold, the heart delays.
In search of warmth, it wanders far,
Beneath the light of the evening star.

The shepherd calls, a gentle sound,
Yet lost in dreams, the silence found.
Each step a prayer, each breath a plea,
In distant lands, the soul seeks free.

Through shadows thick, the heart will roam,
For in the lost, we find our home.
In love's embrace, the weary rest,
The shepherd waits with open chest.

Among the wild, the soul shall rise,
In tender grace, the spirit flies.
With every call, redemption nears,
The lost sheep finds, through love, its tears.

The Hope that Remains

In shadows deep, where silence reigns,
A whisper stirs, not lost in chains.
Faint light emerges, serene and bright,
Guiding hearts through the endless night.

With every prayer that softly soars,
Boundless love opens sacred doors.
Promises linger, like morning dew,
Hope ignites as the soul renews.

In trials faced, though spirits wane,
Resilience blooms amidst the pain.
Each tear we shed, a seed once sown,
In faith, the weary heart finds home.

Let burdens lift, let worries cease,
In gentle hands, we find our peace.
Though storms may rage and shadows fall,
The hope that remains resides in all.

So gather round, in love's embrace,
Together we seek His warm grace.
In every trial, through every strain,
Our hearts will sing, the hope will reign.

A Covenant of Unfulfilled Promises

In ancient texts, the whispers flow,
Of promises made, of seeds to sow.
Yet time moves slow, and visions fade,
In silence, we wait, our faith displayed.

A covenant forged in passion's flame,
Echoes still, yet feels the same.
Longing hearts in shadows dwell,
Awaiting answers, we clasp and swell.

In each unspoken, silent prayer,
We search for signs, for truths laid bare.
Though dreams may falter, and visions stray,
We trust the path will light the way.

In this shared journey, hand in hand,
We seek the promise, a distant land.
With hearts entwined, we stand as one,
For hope survives until we're done.

So hold your faith, in darkness, light,
For every promise shall ignite.
Though unfulfilled, we find our place,
In this covenant of love and grace.

The Blessing of Brokenness

In shattered dreams and fractured ways,
We find the light through darkest days.
A heart laid bare, the truth unveiled,
In brokenness, the spirit's healed.

These scars we bear, each mark a sign,
Of love's embrace, divine, benign.
Through pain we learn, through loss we grow,
In humble prayer, our strengths bestow.

Let every tear drop on the ground,
A sacred gift, where grace is found.
For in our weakness, strength is born,
A blossom blooms, anew each dawn.

The blessing lies in heart's retreat,
Where mercy flows and souls compete.
In letting go, we learn to hold,
The stories of our lives retold.

So cherish each fragment, each small piece,
For brokenness brings forth sweet release.
In every loss, a love remains,
The blessing felt through all life's chains.

Soliloquy of Sorrow

In quiet rooms where memories stir,
The heart whispers low, whispers of her.
Each echo, a tale of joy and ache,
A soliloquy of lessons we take.

Through teary eyes, I gaze within,
Seeking solace where shadows spin.
Each moment lingers, dulcet, deep,
While sorrow sings its song of weep.

In stillness found through tears that flow,
The weight of loss begins to glow.
Embrace the pain, let it unfold,
In heartfelt truths, we find the gold.

For every sorrow teaches grace,
From ashes rise, we find our place.
In longing hearts, a fire burns bright,
A beacon of hope ignites the night.

So let the soul express its plea,
In soliloquy, we seek to be.
With courage found in sorrow's state,
We honor love, we celebrate.

The Altar of Adoration

In the silence of the night, we kneel,
With hearts aglow, to seek and feel.
A sacred space, our whispers rise,
To the heavens, where hope flies.

In humble faith, we bow our heads,
For every word our spirit spreads.
An offering of love, pure and true,
At the altar, we come anew.

The candle's light flickers and sways,
Guiding souls through dusky ways.
In reverence, we speak His name,
In every heartbeat, love's sweet flame.

With gratitude, we lift our voice,
In the presence of God, rejoice.
The echoes of prayer fill the air,
In this moment, we lay bare.

Through the trials, we find our peace,
In divine grace, our fears release.
At the altar, together we'll stand,
Bound in faith, hand in hand.

Tears of a Fallen Angel

Beneath the stars, the shadows creep,
An angel weeps, her heart so steep.
For the dreams that slipped away,
In silence, her longing's sway.

With wings once bright, now dulled by pain,
She mourns for love, in the falling rain.
Each tear a memory, softly shed,
Whispers of hope she once had fed.

A sorrowed hymn fills the night air,
Of lonely journeys and despair.
Yet in the darkness, a spark remains,
A flicker of joy through all the chains.

In brokenness, the spirit finds,
A path to rise, where love unwinds.
Though fallen, she knows she must strive,
To reclaim the light and come alive.

The tears may flow, yet still she flies,
Through trials faced, she lifts her eyes.
For even angels learn to mend,
In the cycle of loss, we ascend.

Hymns of the Brokenhearted

In shadows deep, where sorrow grows,
A broken heart, the pain it shows.
Yet through the cracks, the light shines through,
In every note, a hope anew.

With trembling voice, we sing our pain,
In melodies that softly rain.
Each lyric weaves a fragile thread,
Binding the wounds, where love once bled.

The chorus rises, aching, sweet,
In unity, our hearts do meet.
For in the struggle, we find our song,
Together, we know we belong.

Through hymns of grief, our spirits soar,
In valleys low, we hear love's roar.
From shattered dreams, we build again,
In broken hearts, true strength begins.

In every note, a promise lies,
A blessing born from countless sighs.
For in our hurt, we still believe,
That love endures, and we receive.

The Lamentations of the Unloved

In empty rooms, where silence brews,
A heart aches for the warmth it knew.
Each breath a sigh, a whispered prayer,
In the void, a soul lays bare.

With shadows dancing on the wall,
Loneliness echoes through the hall.
In every corner, memories cling,
Remnants of joy that life once could bring.

Though the world turns, I stand alone,
Seeking love, a heart of stone.
In longing glances, dreams take flight,
Yet fade away into the night.

With tears as ink, I write my fate,
Lamenting softly, filled with weight.
Each verse a tribute to what was lost,
In the name of love, we pay the cost.

But in the shadows, hope remains,
A flickering light through all the pains.
For every heart, though bruised, can heal,
In the depths of love, we will feel.

Chants Under the Veil of Night

In the stillness of the dark, we pray,
Whispers rise to the skies above.
Stars glimmer like souls lost in sin,
Seeking grace with a heart full of love.

Moonlight dances on the sacred ground,
A gentle touch from ethereal hands.
We chant the hymns of the night so deep,
Finding peace in divine commands.

Angels listen to our broken cries,
Each word a plea, each breath a chance.
Under the shroud of the velvet sky,
We surrender in a solemn trance.

The night enfolds our weary souls,
Grant us solace in your light.
Chants under stars that weave our fate,
Guided by faith, we embrace the night.

Together united in fervent prayer,
Hearts aligned with the quiet prayer.
May our troubles fade like shadows in flight,
Chants echo softly, bringing us near.

Redemption in Remorse

Forgive us, Father, our hearts are worn,
In the shadows, regret takes its toll.
We seek redemption, our spirits torn,
Searching for solace to heal our soul.

Tears like rivers flow for the lost,
Each drop a prayer for the choices made.
In the silence, we confront the cost,
In your mercy, let our pasts fade.

Hold us close, dear Lord, in your grace,
For we stumble on this path we tread.
With open hearts, we seek your face,
Lift us up where our spirits led.

In the clasp of hope, we find our way,
Learning to love as we are loved.
Through trials faced, we kneel to pray,
In your embrace, our fears are shoved.

Redemption blooms in the heart of night,
Through remorse, we rise from the dust.
In surrender, we find our light,
With faith restored, we learn to trust.

Eulogies for a Broken Bond

In silence we gather, hearts intertwined,
To mourn the loss of what once was true.
A bond was severed, now undefined,
In echoes of love, we long for you.

Time drifts slowly on the river of tears,
Memories linger in the air of pain.
We eulogize dreams, lost through the years,
Holding on tightly as we try to gain.

The ties that bind now frayed and torn,
Yet in the dark, a flicker ignites.
From ashes of sorrow, hope can be born,
A testament that love still fights.

We light a candle in the night so bleak,
For the moments shared that shaped our way.
In whispers of sorrow, it's love we seek,
A broken bond that will never sway.

Eulogies spoken for what slipped away,
Yet in our hearts, a flicker remains.
Through memories cherished, come what may,
Love's gentle touch, forever sustains.

Atonement in the Ashes

From the ashes of sorrow, we rise anew,
Cleansed by the flames that now set us free.
In the heat of the moment, we see the truth,
Atonement waits, a long, fervent plea.

Transform our hearts, oh divine embrace,
In the embers glow, we seek your face.
Mistakes behind us, we carry the weight,
Yet in your love, we redefine fate.

Forgive our faults, the burdens we bear,
In the still of the night, let grace unfold.
A tapestry woven with threads of despair,
Yet your love shines brightly, more precious than gold.

In surrender, we offer our pain,
From ashes, we build a spirit renewed.
Atonement echoes, no longer in vain,
In the fire's embrace, love's path is viewed.

Guide us, oh Light, through shadows of grief,
In the heart of the storm, our hopes replete.
In the silence, we find our relief,
Atonement in ashes, our faith complete.

Resurrection of the Heart

In shadows cast by doubt's cruel hand,
The heart lies still, like barren land.
But from the depths, a whisper sighs,
Awakening hope, as faith replies.

With every tear, a seed is sown,
In sacred ground, we're never alone.
The sun will rise, the darkness flee,
New life shall bloom, eternally.

Through trials faced, we yearn for grace,
In every struggle, we find Our Place.
A love that binds, so pure and vast,
Reviving souls, our shadows cast.

Embrace the light, let spirits soar,
The heart reborn shall sing once more.
For in the quiet, truth shall reign,
Resurrection breaks the chains of pain.

With open arms, the altar waits,
Infinite mercy that never abates.
In every heartbeat, sacred art,
A journey onward, the Resurrection of the Heart.

Sacrilegious Goodbyes

In whispers soft, we tread the night,
Beneath the stars, we seek the light.
Yet vows once made now fall apart,
Each farewell clings, a broken heart.

The candle flickers, shadows wane,
Silent prayers escape the pain.
What once was holy fades away,
In sacred halls, we dare to stray.

Each sigh, a sin, each glance, a lie,
In the tomb of trust, we softly die.
What angels mourn, the devil keeps,
As love's sweet memory gently sleeps.

We twist the promise, dance with fate,
A sacrilegious choice we hate.
Yet in the depths, the soul's still warm,
Beneath the ash, there's hidden charm.

So let us part, with heavy hearts,
In echoes lost, where silence starts.
For in the pain, we learn to fly,
In every wrong, there's a sacrilegious goodbye.

The Confessional of Lost Dreams

In hollowed space, where whispers dwell,
The curtain drawn, a tangled spell.
With trembling hands, I bare my soul,
In sacred pause, the heart feels whole.

Each dream I cherished, now laid bare,
In shadows deep, hangs silent air.
The hopes I chased, now dust and ash,
In time's embrace, they fade and crash.

With every secret, a weight lifts high,
In truth revealed, I yearn to fly.
The longing echoes, a mournful tune,
In divine light, I face the moon.

Forgive me, Lord, for dreams unsung,
For paths untaken, for battles won.
Yet through the pain, a lesson gleams,
In the confessional of lost dreams.

Hope lingers still, in twilight's grasp,
What once seemed lost, I dare to clasp.
In shadows cast, new visions gleam,
In every heart, a secret dream.

In the Chapel of Longing

In the dim light, shadows dance,
Yearning souls, in a fragile trance.
In hushed whispers, prayers are cast,
In the chapel, we long for the past.

Each candle flickers, a wish, a plea,
For what was lost, for what could be.
Hope hangs heavy, like morning dew,
In sacred stillness, the heart feels true.

Through stained glass, the colors bleed,
A tapestry of every need.
We gather here, our spirits bare,
In the chapel, love fills the air.

A choir echoes, sweet and low,
In every note, our sorrows flow.
The longing swells, a gentle tide,
In this refuge, we must abide.

So let us pray, for dreams reborn,
In the chapel of longing, we mourn.
Yet through our tears, a light will gleam,
In every heart, the spark of a dream.

Candlelight in the Darkness

In shadows deep, the flame does glow,
A beacon bright where spirits flow.
With whispered prayers, we seek the light,
Guided gently through the night.

Each flicker tells a tale of grace,
A promise etched in time and space.
Though trials come, our hearts withstand,
For love will heal, a steady hand.

With faith so pure, we rise anew,
In every stroke, divine and true.
The candle's warmth, a sacred sign,
That hope endures, forever shine.

In pain's embrace, we find our way,
A journey paved in light of day.
So let us hold the flame so dear,
With every heartbeat, love draws near.

Through weary nights, our spirits soar,
For candlelight will guide us more.
In darkness deep, the soul takes flight,
A journey blessed by holy light.

The Gospel of Grief

In sorrow's grip, the heart does ache,
Yet through the pain, we learn to wake.
Each tear a story, a whispered call,
In grief we rise, we do not fall.

The quiet moments, a sacred space,
Where memories linger, love's embrace.
For in the depths of loss, we find,
A gospel sung, to heal the blind.

With heavy hearts, we seek the light,
In every shadow, a new insight.
Though storms may rage and winds may blow,
The bonds of love will always grow.

In every sorrow, a grace unfolds,
The stories of the brave and bold.
Through brokenness, we learn to see,
The strength of faith, our legacy.

Embrace the ache, let spirit soar,
For grief will guide us to the shore.
In unity, we rise again,
A testament to love's refrain.

Faith Beneath the Ashes

From ashes rise, the spirit breathes,
In darkness sown, the heart believes.
The remnants of what once had been,
Give birth to hope, a light within.

Through trials faced, the fire refines,
In grief's deep well, our strength aligns.
With every loss, a thread unwinds,
Yet in the end, our faith binds.

Though storms may rage and chasms yawn,
A new dawn breaks, the night is gone.
In silent prayer, we seek the grace,
That grows from ashes, love's embrace.

With hands uplifted, spirits soar,
Through shadows cast, we seek what's more.
In every trial, a chance to see,
The faith that blooms, eternally.

For from the dust, new life awakes,
In every heartbeat, hope remakes.
With courage fierce, we face the storm,
For faith beneath the ashes warms.

Psalms of Silent Suffering

In silent cries, our hearts refrain,
A song of sorrow, a chord of pain.
Yet in the depths, a whisper stirs,
A hope that lives, though silence blurs.

Each tear a note, each breath a plea,
In faith we find, our spirits free.
Through darkest nights, our souls entwine,
With psalms of love, a grace divine.

Though burdens heavy, hearts may break,
In every trial, a path we take.
We walk with grace, through endless fight,
For in the suffering, we find our light.

With every heartbeat, we learn to trust,
In living waters, we find our dust.
With open arms, we share the pain,
For in the storms, new strength we gain.

In whispered prayers, we search for peace,
In silent suffering, love will cease.
For every song, a bond will stay,
Through psalms of hope, we find our way.

Sanctuaries of Solitude

In the quietude of night,
Whispers echo, soft and light.
In the shadows, peace is found,
Sacred whispers all around.

Beneath the ancient boughs we pray,
Seeking solace day by day.
Heaven's grace, a gentle breeze,
In these moments, hearts find ease.

Each step upon the hallowed ground,
Lost in thoughts, no need for sound.
The stars above, a guiding flame,
In solitude, we call His name.

Nature sings a sacred song,
In these spaces, we belong.
The heart beats with a steady pulse,
In stillness, worship finds its luster.

Awakened souls, with palms held high,
In quiet chambers, spirits fly.
For in each breath, a prayer unfolds,
In sanctuaries, love beholds.

Prayers for a Shattered Spirit

With shards of dreams, we gather here,
Voices tremble, shed a tear.
Heaven's touch upon our plight,
In the darkness, seek the light.

Broken hearts, entwined as one,
Underneath the weeping sun.
Lifted hands, a sacred plea,
Restore our souls, set us free.

In the stillness, faith ignites,
Among the shadows, hope ignites.
Every tear, a silent prayer,
To the heavens, our despair.

Let the winds of mercy flow,
Bring us peace where sorrows go.
In togetherness, we find strength,
In brokenness, we find length.

So we gather, hand in hand,
In this journey, we will stand.
For every prayer, a path reborn,
In shattered spirits, hearts are torn.

Holy Ghosts of Yesterday

Echoes of love from days gone by,
In whispered hymns, we often sigh.
Memories float on timeless streams,
Guided softly by our dreams.

In reflections, the light will bend,
As we search for grace to mend.
Each encounter, a ghostly trace,
In holy moments, we find grace.

As ancient scriptures fill the air,
Lessons learned through deepest care.
In every pause, the past alive,
In sacred veins, our spirits thrive.

We summon forth the tears we've shed,
For in the past, our spirits led.
In every joy and every pain,
The Holy Ghost, our sweet refrain.

Through time's embrace, we dance and weave,
In spirit strong, we still believe.
For yesterday's stories, woven tight,
Guide us gently into the light.

Psalms of a Faded Embrace

In twilight's glow, we seek a sign,
For love once held, now hard to find.
The echoes of a sweet farewell,
In distant chambers, hearts do dwell.

A faded picture on the wall,
Reminds us of the rise and fall.
In gentle reverie, we sigh,
For memories that will not die.

Each tear that falls, a whispered song,
In silence, where our hearts belong.
The rhythm of a love once kind,
Still lingers soft within the mind.

Hands once clasped in unity,
Now reach into the unknown sea.
With faith, we search the dusky skies,
For faded embraces, love complies.

So let us sing the psalms of old,
In elegant tones, our truths retold.
Though love has faded, not erased,
In every shadow, still embraced.

Vestments of a Withered Heart

In shadows deep, the soul does weep,
A garment worn, yet light is torn.
Once vibrant hues, now faded dreams,
In silence, despair's echo screams.

Threads of faith, unraveling slow,
A heart once full, now drowned in woe.
With every prayer, a muted plea,
To mend the fabric, set it free.

Withered blooms, cast aside in grace,
In holy dust, I seek Your face.
Embrace the sorrow, bear the stain,
In vestments tattered, heal the pain.

Lifting hands, the weight I bear,
Each moment fraught, in earnest prayer.
Yet from this ash, a spark may rise,
To find the hope beyond the skies.

Oh, let the dawn bring forth new light,
To breathe on hearts, to banish night.
In withered hearts, Your love ignite,
Thus weaving peace, where darkness bites.

Celestial Desolation

Above the stars, a void so vast,
Where echoes of the lost are cast.
In silent spaces, shadows dwell,
A haunting hymn, a silent bell.

Galaxies spin, yet none remain,
In cosmic dance, we feel the pain.
The breath of worlds, a distant sigh,
In loss profound, we wonder why.

Celestial winds whisper despair,
In solitude, I find my prayer.
Yet still I search the cold abyss,
For solace found in mercy's kiss.

From barren soil, the seeds of hope,
In desolation, I learn to cope.
In every star that fades from sight,
A promise waits to pierce the night.

Beyond the tears, a vision bright,
Emerging from the depth of night.
In celestial realms, I find my way,
Transcending grief, embracing day.

The Anointed Ashes of Us

From embers cold, a bond created,
In ashes deep, our hopes elated.
Together forged, from fire's breath,
Anointed still, though faced with death.

In fragile trust, we seek the light,
Through darkest hours, we hold on tight.
Each tear a testament to love,
Transcending pain, with grace above.

The ashes stir, a sacred dust,
In unity, we place our trust.
With every breath, we rise anew,
In sacred flames, our spirits grew.

Through trials faced, hand in hand,
A journey walked, a promised land.
In the twilight, our shadows blend,
In every moment, find our mend.

So let the fire burn bright and clear,
In anointed ashes, draw You near.
From dust we rise, in love's embrace,
Together bound, our sacred space.

Illumination in the Abyss

In depths where darkness seeds despair,
Where silence wraps its heavy care.
Yet from the void, a whisper stirs,
An illumination, hope occurs.

Through trials deep, my spirit bends,
The weight of sorrow, love transcends.
With trembling hands, I seek the flame,
In shadows cast, yet none to blame.

The abyss calls with chilling breath,
Yet I find light that conquers death.
In every tear, a gem of grace,
Illuminates this hallowed space.

In every sigh, in every thought,
The lessons learned, the battles fought.
A beacon bright amidst the gloom,
In darkest nights, a flower bloom.

Illumination found in pain,
Through trials fierce, our strength we gain.
From depths arise, with spirits free,
In love's embrace, we rise to be.

Divine Echoes of Abandonment

In shadows deep, where silence breathes,
I wander lost, my heart in grief.
The whispers call from heights above,
Yet here I stand, alone in love.

The heavens crack with thunder's hide,
While dreams of faith begin to slide.
Yet still I yearn for bright embrace,
Though I'm forsaken in this place.

The altar warms with tears I shed,
Each prayer a thread to what is dead.
With faith unyielding, I will seek,
The solace strong when spirits speak.

In every loss, a lesson found,
The echoes sing, resound, resound.
And in the void, my spirit grows,
In quiet grace, my heart bestows.

Cherubs Weeping in the Night

Beneath the stars, the cherubs cry,
Their tear drops fall from velvet sky.
In dreams of peace, they mourn the light,
As shadows dance in endless night.

O tender hearts, why wear this pain?
For light shall break through dark's disdain.
With wings of gold, they weep for souls,
In search of love that makes us whole.

The whispers gentle, winds that sigh,
Embrace the lost, the weak, the shy.
In every heart, a longing strong,
To find the place where we belong.

Wait not in sorrow, rise in grace,
Let cherubs guide you to that place.
Where hope ignites and faith is true,
In every tear, a promise new.

Sacrificial Offerings of the Heart

With open hands, I give my all,
Each pulse a plea, each breath a call.
In shadows cast by dreams forlorn,
I find the strength to be reborn.

The altar bears no fragrant gift,
Just humble love, my spirit's lift.
In silence speaks the heart anew,
With tender zeal to see it through.

Through trials faced, I seek the flame,
In every loss, I find the name.
For all that's given, none goes waste,
In sacred acts, I find the grace.

The offering flows from deep within,
A light ignited, beyond sin.
With faith as guide, my path is clear,
Each step a prayer, all doubt to sear.

Reverence in the Ruins

In ruins vast, where echoes dwell,
I wander through the tales they tell.
Of ancient hope and dreams undone,
In sacred time, I find the sun.

The stones are worn, yet wisdom speaks,
In whispered truths, the spirit seeks.
A reverence held for all that's past,
A flicker of light cast far and fast.

In every crack, a heart has bled,
In every silence, prayers once said.
The remnants glow with every tear,
In ruins lives, we draw them near.

The past entwined with what shall come,
In every beat, we find the drum.
With reverence set, my soul is whole,
As shadows fade, I hear the scroll.

Epistles to an Empty Heart

In silence deep, a heart does yearn,
For love divine, to brightly burn.
Each whispered prayer, a fragile plea,
To fill the void, bring hope, set free.

Through valleys dark, where shadows lie,
I seek the light that won't deny.
A longing soul, a fragile thread,
With faith I walk, where angels tread.

Each tear a message, softly sown,
To God above, I am not alone.
In emptiness, my spirit calls,
To find the love that never falls.

With every dawn, new grace I find,
In sorrow sweet, my heart aligned.
For in the stillness, I will dare,
To send my thoughts, to lift my care.

So hear me, Lord, my humble cry,
To mend the heart that longs to fly.
In quiet moments, hope ignites,
Epistles sent into the nights.

Sacred Sorrow

In shadows cast, my spirit weeps,
A sacred sorrow, the heart it keeps.
In trials faced, I walk alone,
Yet in the dark, Your love is shown.

Within the pain, a lesson learned,
In brokenness, the heart has turned.
With every sigh, a prayer I make,
To find the strength in each heartache.

O Blessed One, my guide in night,
Surround me with Your holy light.
In valleys low, Your voice I hear,
A gentle whisper, drawing near.

Through sacred grief, I rise anew,
With open arms, I cling to You.
For in the sorrow, hope will bloom,
In every shadow, love consumes.

So let me weep, for joy shall rise,
Like morning sun in endless skies.
In every tear, a blessing found,
Sacred sorrow, forever bound.

Choirs of the Lonely

In quiet rooms where shadows dwell,
The lonely sing their silent spell.
A chorus born from hearts that ache,
In every note, pure love awake.

With every song, the spirit climbs,
Through sacred spaces, transcending times.
In empty halls, the echoes ring,
A prayerful plea, the angels sing.

Each whispered word, a sacred trust,
To rise above the earth to dust.
In solitude, a strength is found,
In lonely hearts, the world's profound.

So let the choirs of the meek,
Proclaim the love that all hearts seek.
In unity, their voices blend,
A melody that never ends.

For in the lonely, grace takes flight,
A guiding star in darkest night.
In every heart, a song shall start,
Choirs of the lonely, a brand new start.

The Gospel of a Wandering Heart

In restless nights, the heart explores,
A gospel sung by open doors.
With every step, a tale unfolds,
Of love profound, a truth retold.

Across the lands, through seasons change,
The wandering heart finds grace, not strange.
In every trial, a lesson learned,
In every path, a fire burned.

O Traveler, where do you roam?
With every journey, you find home.
In every soul, a spark ignites,
The gospel shared in starry nights.

So take the leap, let faith arise,
For in the wandering, the spirit flies.
Through valleys low and mountains high,
A heart set free, yearning to fly.

In every moment, grace bestowed,
The wandering heart, a sacred road.
With every beat, I sing the song,
Of love divine, to You I belong.

Sacred Solitude in the Wilderness

In the quiet fold of ancient trees,
Whispers of the spirit float like leaves.
With each breath, a prayer unfolds,
Nature's hymn, the heart beholds.

Stars above in reverent gaze,
Illuminate the winding ways.
In solitude, the soul does merge,
With the wild, divine aturge.

Every brook sings sacred tones,
Echoing through the valley's bones.
Among the rocks, the truth is cast,
In wilderness, the peace steadfast.

Mountains stand where shadows play,
Guardians of the night and day.
In their silence, wisdom found,
A presence felt, profound, unbound.

Alone yet never truly lone,
In the breath of earth, I've grown.
With every step, the spirit's dance,
Invites the heart to take its chance.

Liturgies of Emptiness

Within the hollowed space of mind,
Where echoes of the lost can bind.
Each thought released, an empty prayer,
In silence deep, divinity's stare.

In the cavern of a barren soul,
Lies the seed of a greater whole.
To let go is to be reborn,
In the void, the heart adorn.

Fasting from desire's sweet embrace,
The spirit finds its sacred place.
In surrender, we find the light,
Emerging from the darkest night.

Shadows fade in the glow of grace,
Chiseled by time, we find our space.
Communion with the nothingness,
Holds the key to the eternal bliss.

Liturgies of the void declared,
In stillness, the heart prepared.
For in emptiness, love expands,
Binding grace with gentle hands.

The Calling of a Scorned Heart

A heart once bruised in shadows cast,
Yearns for the light, a glow steadfast.
In bitter winds, the spirit calls,
To rise anew beyond the falls.

Scorned by the world, yet not alone,
In every ache, the seeds are sown.
From brokenness comes strength divine,
A symphony of life's design.

Through the veil of wounds and tears,
The voice of hope rings clear, it cheers.
In every wound, a story sings,
Of healing touched by sacred wings.

So heed the call; the journey starts,
From ashes of the scorned hearts.
With faith, we weave our tapestry,
In love, we forge our legacy.

Open your soul to the vast unknown,
In surrender, the truth is grown.
Embrace the scars, let them impart,
The wisdom of a scorned heart.

Ashes to Ascendancy

From ashes rise the dreams once burned,
In the furnace of life, lessons learned.
Each fragment glows with hope reborn,
In the twilight of the early morn.

The weight of sorrow gently shed,
As wings unfurl where angels tread.
In the embers of despair's own fire,
A phoenix soars; it dares aspire.

With every tear, the soul ignites,
Transforming pain to guiding lights.
In the dance of loss, we find our grace,
To rise again and embrace the space.

Through trials faced and battles fought,
We claim the strength that life has taught.
From sorrow's depth, the spirit gleams,
In ashes, boundless are our dreams.

Ascendancy, the journey's claim,
In hearts ablaze, we find the flame.
So rise anew with courage blessed,
From ashes, rise, forever pressed.

The Last Prayer for Us

In shadows deep, we find our plea,
A whisper soft, a hope to see.
With humble hearts, we seek the light,
In darkest hours, our souls take flight.

We gather here, in sacred space,
To turn our scars into grace.
With open arms, we face the dawn,
Together strong, we carry on.

Oh, weary souls, we lift our gaze,
Through trials faced, we sing Your praise.
In every tear, a lesson grows,
In love's embrace, the spirit flows.

Each prayer we offer, pure and true,
In every heartbeat, we find You.
With every breath, we strive to be,
A testament of unity.

So guide us, Lord, through tempest seas,
Fill our hearts with gentle ease.
In final words, we trust in grace,
As we surrender, find our place.

Testament of Teardrops

Each teardrop falls, a tale untold,
A testament where hearts unfold.
In sorrow's grip, we seek to mend,
In fragile moments, love transcends.

Through valleys low, our spirits ache,
Yet in the pain, new paths we make.
With every tear, a strength we find,
In weary hearts, new hope aligned.

Remember those who walked with grace,
With gentle hands, they held our space.
In every sigh, a prayer released,
A love profound that never ceased.

Oh, grief will come but so will joy,
In life's grand weave, we find our buoy.
Through every loss, a flame ignites,
A testament through darkest nights.

So cherish tears, let them flow free,
For in their depths, we come to see.
In every drop, a story clear,
A legacy of love held dear.

Soliloquy of the Unheard

In whispered winds, our voices rise,
A soliloquy beneath the skies.
For silent cries and dreams untold,
In hidden hearts, the truth unfolds.

We walk among the lost and meek,
In every glance, the stories speak.
With every sigh and every breath,
We find the strength to conquer death.

Oh, unvoiced souls, do not despair,
In shadows cast, we find our prayer.
In moments small, in quiet grace,
The echoes of the heart embrace.

Through love unspoken, we take flight,
In darkness deep, we seek the light.
In every corner, joy and strife,
We weave the fabric of our life.

So hear this call, the truth be known,
In silence shared, we find our own.
Together strong, we raise our cry,
In unity, we learn to fly.

The Good Book of Goodbye

In every chapter, we learn to say,
A fond farewell at the close of day.
With heavy hearts, we turn the page,
In love, we find our sacred gauge.

Goodbyes are not the end, but start,
A journey carved within the heart.
In memories woven, we reside,
In whispered dreams where love abides.

We honor those who came before,
In every smile, we feel their core.
Through lessons learned and laughter shared,
A legacy of love declared.

So hold the moments, cherish time,
In every sunset, a quiet rhyme.
With every goodbye, we find a way,
To honor love that will not sway.

In gratitude, we raise our eyes,
To every bond that never dies.
In the good book, these words reside,
A testament to love and pride.

The Wandering Disciple of Love

In shadows cast by ancient trees,
A heart set free from earthly ties.
With every step, a soft embrace,
The spirit soars, the soul complies.

He wanders far, through fields of grace,
With gentle whispers, love's embrace.
Each lesson learned, a sacred vow,
To spread His light in every place.

Through trials faced, the path is clear,
In solitude, the truth draws near.
A faithful heart, a guiding star,
In every choice, His love appears.

The world may judge with fleeting glances,
But faith ignites the soul's advances.
In simple acts, divinity,
Through love, the heart forever dances.

A disciple lost, yet ever found,
In every heartbeat, love profound.
With every tear, a promise blooms,
His presence felt, in joy unbound.

Grace in the Face of Grief

In quiet moments, shadows blend,
The heart reflects on scenes we tend.
With heavy burdens, spirits rise,
For love endures, it will not bend.

In sorrow's arms, we seek His face,
A gentle touch, a warm embrace.
Through tears that fall like softest rain,
We find in grief, a holy grace.

Each memory sings a sacred tune,
In darkest nights, we see the moon.
With every heartbeat, hope ignites,
A guiding light through deepest gloom.

The past, a tapestry so grand,
Woven tight by His own hand.
In every thread, a story told,
Of love that flourished, like the sand.

With faith restored, we lift our eyes,
To skies where love never dies.
In grace we walk, though hearts may ache,
For in His arms, forever lies.

Sins of Sweet Remembrance

In whispers soft, the past awakes,
With every choice, the heart it breaks.
An echo lingers, sweet yet sad,
In moments shared, a love partakes.

The memories dance like fleeting stars,
In every laugh, and all the scars.
We hold them close, these fleeting sins,
In shadows cast by love's memoirs.

A fleeting glance, a touch divine,
Each sin a poem, a sacred line.
In the tapestry, our hearts entwine,
Reminding us of love's design.

Through time, we wander, lost yet found,
In the sweetest sins, our hearts rebound.
For every tear that gently falls,
A promise made, our souls unbound.

In every heartbeat, love remains,
In sacred bonds and soft refrains.
Though sins may haunt with gentle grace,
Their beauty lies in what sustains.

Broken Rosaries and Forgotten Dreams

With strings unbound and beads undone,
A prayer once whispered now is gone.
In broken faith, the heart does yearn,
For dreams once bright, now overrun.

Yet in the silence, echoes sound,
Of hope reborn, where love is found.
Each fragment tells a tale of pain,
In every loss, a grace profound.

Through shadows deep, the spirit cries,
For every tear, a question lies.
Yet in the cracks, new light shall rise,
To guide the heart to clearer skies.

The rosary, though worn and frayed,
Still holds the faith that never fades.
In every whispered prayer we weave,
A strength emerges, unafraid.

In dreams forgotten, seeds are sown,
In barren fields, new life is grown.
With every prayer, a fresh embrace,
As hope returns, our hearts have flown.

Sacrament of Silent Tears

In whispered prayers we find our grace,
Each drop a story, a sacred trace.
Beneath the weight of sorrow's light,
We seek the dawn, we yearn for night.

In shadows cast by heavy hearts,
Our tears like rivers, they play their parts.
A sacrament of grief declared,
In silence deep, our hopes laid bare.

With every sorrow, a lesson learned,
In every tear, a soul discerned.
The holy balm of shared lament,
In unity, all hearts are bent.

The altar built from pain and woe,
Where silence speaks, and love can grow.
Together in this sacred space,
We weave our tears with gentle grace.

So let each silent tear we pour,
Be sacrament forevermore.
In every drop, a faith reborn,
In every sorrow, love is worn.

The Last Communion of Lost Love

In twilight's glow, love's shadows fall,
A final pledge to heed the call.
The cup is filled with bitter fate,
In every sip, we contemplate.

As memories linger, soft yet frayed,
The echoes linger, serenely laid.
In every glance, a promise kept,
In every sigh, our hearts have wept.

Communion held in silent trust,
A bond now cracked, reduced to dust.
Yet in the stillness, whispers say,
True love will never fade away.

The bread we break, both sweet and sour,
In every hour, we mourn our flower.
Though lost to time, the heart must grieve,
In every loss, there's more to weave.

In dusky hues of fading light,
We share this pain, we share the night.
Let reverent silence guide our souls,
As we embrace what once was whole.

Pilgrimage Through Empty Temples

We wander through the hollow halls,
Where echoes of the past still call.
Each step a whisper, lost in time,
In sacred spaces, we seek the sublime.

The altar stands, adorned with dust,
In prayers unspoken, we place our trust.
Among the shadows, spirits roam,
In every crack, we find our home.

A pilgrimage of heart's intent,
Through empty temples, we are sent.
Each quiet room holds stories grand,
In whispered faith, we make our stand.

The stained glass weeps with colors bright,
As sunlight filters, bringing light.
We kneel and bow, our heads in prayer,
In every silence, a sacred care.

With every step, we shed our fears,
In every tear, we find the years.
A journey long, yet ever near,
Through empty temples, love is clear.

Hymns of Hollow Souls

In the stillness, shadows dwell,
Echoes of a forgotten bell.
We raise our voices, soft and low,
In hymns that only silence knows.

A chorus bent with heavy sighs,
The cries of souls who've said goodbyes.
In hollow hearts, the music swells,
A testament in whispered spells.

Each note a prayer, each tone a plea,
In yearning hearts, we seek to be.
The hymns of love, the loss extends,
In every chord, a message sends.

Together in this sacred song,
We find a place where we belong.
Though hollowed, still our spirits soar,
In harmony, forevermore.

So let the hymns of hollow souls,
Resound and echo, making whole.
In every heart, a song to sing,
In every loss, new hope will spring.

Chasing Light Through Desolation

In shadows deep, where sorrows dwell,
We seek the dawn, our hearts to swell.
With faith as our guide, we tread the night,
Chasing grace, embracing light.

Through barren lands, where hope seems lost,
We find the warmth, no matter the cost.
In every tear, a spark ignites,
Leading us closer to sacred heights.

For in the gloom, a whisper calls,
Promising joy when the darkness falls.
With every step, a prayer ascends,
Revealing love that never ends.

When tempests rage and doubts are near,
In quiet moments, we find Him here.
With open hearts and spirits wide,
We chase the light, our faithful guide.

So let us rise, with voices clear,
Proclaiming hope for all who hear.
In desolation, we stand as one,
Chasing the light, until we're done.

A Prayer for the Weary

O Lord, in times of weary strife,
We lift our hearts, our hopes, our life.
In silent prayer, we seek Your grace,
To find our strength in Your embrace.

When burdens weigh and spirits fall,
We call on You to hear our call.
Like gentle rain on thirsty ground,
In Your love, our peace is found.

In moments dark, when shadows loom,
We feel Your light dispel the gloom.
With every doubt that clouds our mind,
Your tender mercy, we will find.

So guide us through the troubled days,
And fill our hearts with songs of praise.
In every trial, let courage rise,
We trust in You, our hope, our prize.

With faith renewed, we stand upright,
A prayer for strength, a yearning light.
In midnight's hour, we won't despair,
For You are always with us there.

Sins of the Beloved

In shadows cast by love's great light,
We wrestle with our flaws, our plight.
Each choice we make, a burden born,
The heart that loves can be so torn.

Yet in our sins, Your love breaks through,
Forgiveness flows, our souls renew.
For in the depths of our disgrace,
Your mercy laws time and space.

With every fall, we rise again,
O Beloved, through joy and pain.
In sacred trust, we learn to see,
The grace that flows so endlessly.

You hold our hearts, no shame remains,
In Your embrace, we shed our chains.
Though we may stumble, we shall rise,
In love's reflection, truth implies.

So let us walk with heads held high,
Through trials faced, we learn to fly.
O Beloved, in Your name we stand,
Redeemed and free, by Your own hand.

Sacred Echoes of Solitude

In solitude, we hear the call,
A whisper through the silent hall.
With every breath, a sacred pause,
In stillness found, we feel the cause.

Amidst the noise of worldly chase,
We find our peace, our sacred space.
In humble hearts, devotion grows,
Through quietude, Your presence flows.

O Lord, in solitude, we pray,
To light our path, to guide our way.
In every moment, still and true,
We seek the face that shines anew.

With open hearts, we hear You speak,
In silent moments, strong yet meek.
Your love, a balm for weary souls,
In sacred echoes, we find wholeness.

So let us cherish every hour,
In solitude, we feel Your power.
Embracing peace, in quiet light,
We find our strength, our sacred sight.

The Fellowship of Fallen Petals

In gardens where the whispers dwell,
Petals fall like stories told,
Each one a prayer, a silent spell,
In colors vivid, shades of gold.

Amidst the blooms, a fellowship grows,
A sacred bond in nature's grace,
Where each soft petal, gently flows,
To find its place in time and space.

With every dusk, the shadows fade,
Yet beauty lingers, never lost,
For in the heart, a love is made,
A testament to what it costs.

In every tear that plants this earth,
There lies a story of pure light,
From fallen petals, springs new birth,
In darkness gifted, shines the bright.

So let us gather, one and all,
In reverence of the fallen grace,
Together in the petals' call,
We trace our path, we find our place.

Monuments to Forgotten Love

In silent chambers of the night,
Stand monuments to love once held,
Each stone a memory, pure and bright,
In echoes where the heart has dwelled.

We build with tears and laughter sweet,
A legacy of warmth and pain,
Though time may tread with heavy feet,
These structures hold our joy and strain.

With every sunset, shadows play,
On markers of the days gone by,
In dreams we wander and we pray,
For love that felt as vast as sky.

Yet in the chill of twilight's song,
These monuments stand tall and proud,
They speak of bonds that were so strong,
In whispers soft, amidst the crowd.

So let us cherish what we've shared,
For in each stone, a heart does beat,
With every love, we are ensnared,
A tale of loss, but fondly sweet.

Anathemas of Affection

In shadows cast by love's own hand,
Anathemas in fervent hearts,
Whispers echo in the quiet land,
As passion weaves its tangled arts.

What once was sweet now stings the soul,
A fragile web of dreams undone,
In broken vows, we pay the toll,
A dance of light and dark begun.

Through trials fierce, our spirits learn,
The cost of love, a bitter price,
Yet even in the wounds that burn,
Resilience sparks and blooms like rice.

For every heart that bears the pain,
A deeper well of wisdom grows,
Through anathemas, we find the gain,
In storms, the gentle spirit flows.

So let us not in darkness dwell,
But rise from ashes, strong and free,
For in the depths, we forge a spell,
That turns our wounds to empathy.

Fables of the Fallen

In tales of old, the fallen sing,
Of battles fought and love's embrace,
Each fable wrapped in sacred ring,
A story carved in time and space.

Through winding paths the spirits tread,
With hearts aflame, they seek the truth,
In every verse, the tears they shed,
Bear witness to the pain of youth.

In shadows long, their echoes call,
Reminders of the paths once taken,
From heights of joy to depths of fall,
In every heart, a dream awakened.

Yet in each fable, hope remains,
For in the sorrow, lessons grow,
Through trials faced and endless pains,
A seed of faith begins to show.

So gather round, and learn their lore,
In fables whispered on the breeze,
For every tale opens a door,
To finding peace amidst the seas.

Revelations of a Shattered Spirit

In shadows deep, the heart does cry,
A whisper of hope, a silent sigh.
The broken glass reflects the light,
In darkness found, the soul takes flight.

The heavens weep, the stars seem near,
A sacred promise quells the fear.
In every tear, a truth unfolds,
A story written, forever told.

The ashes speak of battles fought,
Lessons learned, and beauty sought.
Through trials faced, the spirit bends,
Yet in the end, the journey mends.

The light breaks through, a divine embrace,
In shattered realms, we find our place.
For every loss a blessing waits,
Revelations born of heavy fates.

With open hearts, we rise anew,
In faith and love, the world's a view.
The shattered spirit finds its song,
In unity, we all belong.

The Serpent of Suffering

In the garden of life, shadows creep,
Where whispers of anguish softly seep.
The serpent coils, with venomous grace,
Temptation's kiss, a painful embrace.

Beneath the scales lies a heart so cold,
A tale of sorrow, eternally told.
In every wound, a lesson burns,
For every fall, a chance returns.

Yet in the grasp of despair's tight hold,
A spark ignites, a spirit bold.
In suffering's grip, we find our truth,
The inner child, the eternal youth.

With battles fought and scars so deep,
We learn to sow the seeds we reap.
The serpent guides through pain's embrace,
To depths of soul, we find our grace.

And bound together in pain we rise,
With eyes wide open to the skies.
The serpent's song becomes our hymn,
In suffering's arms, our hearts don't dim.

Cherubs in the Ruins

Amongst the crumbling stones we tread,
Where echoes of the past are fed.
Cherubs dance in the dust and grime,
In broken halls, they bide their time.

With wings outstretched, they whisper low,
Of love and peace in the undertow.
In every crack, a glimmer glows,
From ashes sprout, the hope that grows.

Though ruins whisper tales of woe,
The cherubs sing of seeds we sow.
From pain emerges joy anew,
In shattered places, grace breaks through.

With tender hearts, we grasp the thread,
Of beauty found where fears have led.
In every ruin, a lesson gleams,
Cherubs remind us of love's dreams.

For in the rubble, life reclaims,
The sacred dance, the sacred names.
Through every trial, we find the way,
Cherubs in ruins, guide our stay.

Ascending Through the Abyss

In the depths of night, where shadows dwell,
We seek the light, a sacred spell.
The abyss calls with its chilling breath,
Yet through its depths, we conquer death.

With each step forward, fear recedes,
In every heartbeat, a spirit leads.
Through trials faced, we learn to soar,
In the darkest hours, we find our core.

The twilight whispers of dreams untold,
A path of faith, both fierce and bold.
With courage as our guiding star,
We emerge from shadows, near and far.

In the silent echoes, strength is found,
A symphony of hope resounds.
The abyss may linger, but we ascend,
With hearts ablaze, on faith depend.

Though darkness looms, we rise with grace,
Through trials endured, we find our place.
Ascending through, the light we greet,
In the journey whole, our spirits meet.

The Ascendance of Solitary Prayers

In the silence, hearts will sigh,
Seeking solace in the sky.
Words unspoken, hopes arise,
Faith like whispers, never dies.

Beneath the stars, a silent plea,
Each tear a bridge to the decree.
Faithful shadows, night and light,
Guiding souls through darkest night.

Voices rise on winds of grace,
In solitude, we find our place.
With every breath, a sacred quest,
In solitude, we are blessed.

When faith feels faint, and doubts intrude,
In silent prayers, our hearts renewed.
Each longing soul holds the key,
To unlock heaven's mystery.

On mountains high, in valleys deep,
In whispered vows, the secrets keep.
Ascend the heights where spirits soar,
In solitude, we are evermore.

Chasing Miracles in Shadows

In the twilight, shadows play,
Chasing miracles that sway.
Glimmers of hope in the night,
Holding dreams, hearts take flight.

With every step, a prayer spoken,
From the depths, our fears unbroken.
Faith that dances, light entwined,
In the darkness, love refined.

Underneath the moon's soft glow,
We seek the signs that heaven shows.
Each breath a step, each sigh a chance,
To waltz with life in sacred dance.

In the stillness, whispers call,
Guiding us when shadows fall.
Miracles weave a gentle thread,
Binding hearts where hopes are fed.

Among the stars, the truth we chase,
Finding grace in every space.
In shadows deep, find the spark,
Chasing miracles in the dark.

Echoes of Empty Ceremonies

In hallowed halls, silence lingers,
Echoing words with ghostly fingers.
Rituals fade where shadows creep,
Empty ceremonies sow what we reap.

Candles burn in quiet prayer,
Lingering scents fill the air.
Voices once bright, now but a sigh,
In the stillness, memories die.

Bells that rang from towers high,
Now whisper soft, a muted cry.
Echoes linger of love once shared,
In a space where hearts were bared.

Yet hope persists in the cold night,
In the echoes, find the light.
Amidst the stillness, souls may find,
A spark of grace, forever blind.

In the ashes, stories remain,
Of love and loss, of joy and pain.
An empty seat, a silent prayer,
Echoes of life linger in the air.

Divine Parables of Abandonment

In shadows deep, a story breathes,
Of love unshared, of hearts that grieve.
Lessons taught in silence loud,
In abandonment, we are avowed.

Like whispers lost in the storm's embrace,
Hearts abandoned seek their place.
Yet through the pain, a truth reveals,
In brokenness, the spirit heals.

The lonely road, a path of grace,
Where human hearts find their space.
Every tear a tear of prayer,
In solitude, we learn to care.

In every loss, a lesson shines,
Divine parables, sacred signs.
When darkness falls and hope feels faint,
Hearts once broken become a saint.

So rise, dear soul, from depths of woe,
In abandonment, let love grow.
For even in the darkest night,
Divine light comes, a guiding sight.

The Crucible of Lingering Longing

In shadows cast by yearning souls,
We search for grace, we ache for whole.
Each whispered prayer a sacred plea,
To find the light, to set us free.

With heavy hearts, we tread the path,
Through trials deep, enduring wrath.
In every tear, a lesson learned,
In every flame, a candle burned.

The dawn arrives with promises,
Of hope reborn in endless bliss.
In love's embrace, we find our way,
Through darkest nights, to brightest day.

Yet shadows linger, doubts collide,
In this crucible, we coincide.
Awake our souls, ignite the fire,
For in our longing, we aspire.

Together we'll rise, unbound by chains,
In faith and trust, our love remains.
Through trials faced, we shall not fall,
In the crucible, we conquer all.

Candles in the Wind of Despair

In flickering flames, our hopes reside,
Against the storm, we will abide.
With every gust, we lift in prayer,
Our candles glow, though filled with care.

When darkness whispers, chill and drear,
We kindle light, dissolve the fear.
Through rustling leaves, our spirits soar,
In faith, we find forevermore.

Each flame a beacon, brave and bold,
With stories of the truth retold.
We find our strength in love's embrace,
In every trial, we seek His grace.

Though winds may howl, and shadows fall,
Together we rise, we heed the call.
In solidarity, we stand true,
Candles lit, the dark we'll subdue.

As night takes hold, we shall not fear,
For in each heart, the light is near.
With every breath, our spirits climb,
In the wind of despair, we shine.

Missionaries of Memories

In every heartbeat, a story told,
Of love and loss, of hearts of gold.
We carry forth these tales divine,
As missionaries, we intertwine.

With open arms, we share the tears,
We heal the wounds, we calm the fears.
In whispered joys, and silent cries,
We breathe the truth, and never lie.

Through golden sunsets, our souls ignite,
In cherished moments, bathed in light.
Together we weave a tapestry,
Of memories etched eternally.

In every smile, a promise made,
In love's embrace, our doubts allayed.
As missionaries, we spread the peace,
In unity, our spirits cease.

The legacy we choose to share
Is stitched with love, beyond compare.
For in this journey, we are blessed,
Missionaries of memories, we rest.

The Last Supper of Togetherness

In gathering close, we build our dreams,
At the table laid, where love redeems.
With every bite, connections grow,
In laughter, tears, our spirits flow.

The bread we break, a symbol grand,
With shared intentions, hand in hand.
Each sip a promise, strong and true,
In this communion, we renew.

As fragrant meals grace our night,
We cherish moments, pure delight.
The warmth of voices, soft and clear,
In the last supper, we draw near.

Together we rise, unyielding fate,
In trust and love, we celebrate.
As families blend, in harmony,
The table set for unity.

When dishes fade and candles burn low,
The spirit lingers, in hearts it glows.
For in togetherness, we find our place,
At the last supper, a touch of grace.

Tainted Benedictions

In whispered prayers of fleeting grace,
The hands that reach are stained by sin.
Yet still we seek the sacred space,
Where mercy's light can pull us in.

The altar stands, a witness worn,
Upon its stone, our burdens lay.
With every tear, our souls are torn,
In search for peace along the way.

These benedictions, frail and weak,
A longing heart with hope commands.
In struggles deep, we dare to speak,
Yearning for love with open hands.

Yet shadows creep where faith once shone,
The taint of doubt hangs like a shroud.
Do we remain, or walk alone,
Our voices lost within the crowd?

Let us rise, though weak and frail,
To seek the path where mercy leads.
In every trial, in every gale,
We find the strength in whispered creeds.

Seraphic Shadows of What Was

In visions grand, the angels fall,
Their wings embrace the dawn of time.
Yet memories whisper soft and small,
Of moments lost in endless rhyme.

Once bright, the temple stood so tall,
With light that danced upon the walls.
Now echoes linger, cold and small,
As silence deep within us calls.

Seraphic shadows sway and blend,
In twilight's hold, where dreams fade slow.
Each heartbeat marks a sacred end,
As we recall the grace we know.

In prayer's embrace, we seek the past,
To find the love that guides our way.
Each fleeting thought, forever cast,
In hope's embrace, we long to stay.

Yet in the dark, the light remains,
A flicker in the depths of night.
In sorrow's fold, through all the pains,
A seraph's song returns our flight.

Hymn of the Forsaken

We gather here, the lost, the meek,
In shadows cast by judgment's hand.
With hearts once pure, now torn and weak,
We search for grace in barren land.

The hymn we sing, a sorrowed tune,
Of souls adrift in night's despair.
Yet still, beneath the waning moon,
The hope of dawn hangs in the air.

Forsaken paths we tread alone,
With heavy hearts, we lift our eyes.
In every tear, a seed is sown,
To bloom anew beneath the skies.

With every note, our spirits rise,
In unity, though torn apart.
In timeless grace the truth belies,
A love that mends the wounded heart.

Together, bound by faith, we stand,
In echoes of the ages past.
Our voices rise, a faithful band,
In joy, our sorrows fall at last.

Altar of Lost Promises

Upon this stone, the vows once made,
Lie shattered like the dreams they bore.
In solemn tones, the past won't fade,
Yet still, we strive to seek once more.

The altar stands where hope did bloom,
Its beauty stained with shadows cast.
We come to mourn, to lift the gloom,
And find the strength to face the past.

In whispered prayers, our fate entwined,
We reach for grace with trembling hearts.
Though lost, our way remains defined,
By love that never truly departs.

With images of what we sought,
Upon this ground, we lay our tears.
For every promise, pale and fraught,
We build anew despite our fears.

In burning flame, our spirits rise,
As ashes fall in winds of time.
The altar speaks, no more the lies,
We claim our strength through love's divine.

Suffering Saints of the Past

In shadows deep, where faith was tried,
Saints walked paths of pain and pride.
With heavy hearts, they bore the loss,
Yet found in tears, the sacred cross.

Their whispers linger, a soft refrain,
Through trials faced and endless pain.
In night's despair, they sought the light,
With broken dreams, they reached for sight.

Hand in hand, they journeyed far,
Their faith a beacon, a guiding star.
In every wound, a story told,
Of love unyielding, of strength bold.

In quiet moments, their spirits rise,
To touch the heavens, to part the skies.
They paved the way, with steadfast grace,
In suffering's depths, they found their place.

With each step taken, they bore the cost,
In the garden of anguish, they found the lost.
Their legacy, a holy ground,
In sorrow's grip, true hope was found.

Hope's Dying Flame

In distant embers, hope flickers low,
A fragile light in the midst of woe.
Yet still it dances, against the night,
A testament to the inner fight.

With weary hearts, we lift our gaze,
Through darkness thick, we seek to blaze.
For even when shadows stretch so wide,
The spark within shall ever abide.

In whispered prayers, we keep it warm,
A beating heart against the storm.
Through ashes cold, the truth remains,
A promise veiled in sacred strains.

When hope seems lost, within the pain,
We breathe the fire, we fan the flame.
For every trial we must embrace,
Leads to a brighter, holy place.

In quiet moments, grace will sing,
To lift us up on gentle wing.
Though flames may flicker, they shall not die,
For in our hearts, hope learns to fly.

Voices of the Emptied

From hollow shells, the voices call,
In empty rooms where shadows fall.
With echoes soft, they weave their pain,
In silence rich, a sacred refrain.

Each word released, a tear unshed,
Tales of longing, of love once bred.
They haunt the halls of memory's keep,
Awakening dreams from restless sleep.

In whispered truths, they find their way,
Through cracks of night into the day.
For emptiness holds a sacred space,
Where souls connect in a warm embrace.

Amidst the sorrow, hope softly sighs,
In every heart, a spark that tries.
The voices blend, a harmony sweet,
In unity's song, they find their feet.

Through every shadow, they break the chain,
In shared lament, they forge the gain.
As echoes linger, love's truth is known,
In empty spaces, we're not alone.

The Spirit's Lament

Oh spirit weary, in silence you weep,
In restless nights, your burden so deep.
With every sigh, a prayer takes flight,
To find the dawn in darkest night.

In fields of sorrow, you wander lost,
The weight of sorrow, the heavy cost.
Yet in your tears, there blooms a rose,
A testament to strength that grows.

With gentle whispers, the heartache sings,
Of healing hope and brighter things.
In every trial, a lesson learned,
In faith's embrace, the spirit burned.

Through valleys deep, the tears will flow,
In sacred sadness, the spirit knows.
For every lament, a hymn shall rise,
To touch the heavens, to pierce the skies.

O spirit bright, your song will soar,
In quiet moments, forevermore.
For in your ache, there lies the truth,
A love eternal, a sacred youth.

Beneath the Stained Glass of Grief

Beneath the stained glass of grief,
We gather in silence and prayer,
Seeking solace from our sorrow,
In the light of love laid bare.

Through colors that weep and blend,
We find the stories of the lost,
Echoing whispers in the dark,
Reminding us of the cost.

The candles flicker, hearts ignite,
In moments of quiet despair,
In the beauty of fractured dreams,
We lift our burdens in the air.

With every breath, we forge a bond,
In the embrace of shared lament,
Together we weave our memories,
Finding strength in the time we spent.

And under the watch of the heavens,
We rise as the shadows recede,
Beneath the stained glass of hope,
We carry love's eternal seed.

Embracing the Cross of Loss

In the quiet of night's embrace,
We find the weight of our sorrow,
Clutching tightly to the cross,
Dreaming of a brighter tomorrow.

Each tear that falls like rain,
Is a prayer whispered to the skies,
In the pain we share as one,
Resilience in our goodbyes.

Love is a light in darkest times,
Guiding us through storms of despair,
With faith as our steady anchor,
We grasp the strength in our prayers.

As we walk this path together,
Embracing the ache and the grace,
We lift our hearts in unity,
Finding peace in love's embrace.

In the dawn of each new day,
We honor those who've passed and gone,
Embracing the cross of loss,
Transcending the night with song.

The Temple of Unspoken Words

Deep within the temple walls,
Lie the echoes of our hearts,
Whispers caught on ancient stone,
Unspoken truths that tear apart.

In shadows where silence dwells,
We gather our fears and dreams,
Offering them to the divine,
In the quiet, hope redeems.

Each sigh a prayer, each glance a plea,
In the space where souls align,
We learn the art of listening,
To the voice within, so divine.

With every heartbeat, we express,
What words cannot begin to share,
In the temple of unbroken trust,
We find the grace in our despair.

Here we build with love and faith,
A sanctuary made of light,
The temple of unspoken words,
Guiding us through darkest night.

Broken Altars of Desire

On broken altars of desire,
We place our hopes and fears,
In the ashes of what once burned,
The weight of countless years.

Each fragment tells a story,
Of love that sought to soar,
Yet grounded by life's burdens,
Longing for something more.

In prayer, we mend the pieces,
With faith as our guiding star,
Finding beauty in the cracks,
In the lessons from afar.

Amid the ruins of our wants,
New seeds of grace will bloom,
From broken altars rise the light,
Dissolving all our gloom.

Let us gather here together,
With hearts laid bare in trust,
From broken altars of desire,
We rise, we love, we must.

The Visions of a Forsaken Heart

In shadows deep, the heart does weep,
Whispers of love in silence keep.
Faith once bright, now dimmed by plight,
Yearning for light in endless night.

A prayer rises, like smoke in air,
Desires entwined in a frozen prayer.
Hope's fragile thread begins to fray,
Lost in the echoes of yesterday.

The soul reflects on paths untried,
Wonders where innocence had died.
Distant stars seem cold and far,
Guiding but never what they are.

Yet from the ashes, embers glow,
A flicker of faith begins to grow.
The heart seeks mercy, pure and bright,
Craving the warmth of divine light.

Oh, forsaken heart, rise once more,
Feel the whisper from heaven's floor.
See the visions, lost yet near,
Embrace the love that casts out fear.

Grace in the Wake of Silence

In stillness found, the soul does sigh,
Beneath the watchful, starry sky.
Grace that flows like a gentle stream,
Fills the heart with a sacred dream.

In moments hushed, the spirit soars,
Across the vast, celestial shores.
Each breath a prayer, each thought a song,
Guided by what feels so wrong.

The silence speaks in tender tones,
Reminding us we're not alone.
In echoes soft, the heart can mend,
Finding solace in a friend.

As shadows retreat, the dawn draws near,
Embracing all that we hold dear.
With every heartbeat, grace reveals,
The love of God, a truth that heals.

Awake within the quiet space,
To know that silence holds His grace.
In stillness, hearts begin to dance,
In reverent awe, we take our chance.

The Divine Dance of Departure

In sacred twilight, shadows blend,
A journey starts, where souls ascend.
The veil between now drifts away,
As angels lead the hearts that sway.

With every step, the spirits rise,
Entering realms beyond the skies.
A dance of joy, of bittersweet,
In timeless circles, hearts do meet.

Each farewell echoes with grace profound,
In love's embrace, we're tightly bound.
The divine sighs as we take flight,
To realms unknown, embraced by light.

In twilight's glow, the past laid bare,
The burdens lifted, free to care.
We move with trust, though paths unseen,
The dance of life flows, serene and keen.

O wondrous journey, tender and bold,
In every story, love unfolds.
With every tear, a star will shine,
Guiding the steps of the divine.

Mourning in the Temple

In the temple's heart, shadows dwell,
Whispers carry a mournful spell.
Candles flicker, souls laid bare,
Seeking solace in heavy air.

With every chime, the heart beats slow,
Lost in grief, our tears will flow.
In this sacred space, we pray,
For those we've lost, who've gone away.

The walls hold stories, echoes deep,
Of promises made and those who weep.
Each corner whispers forgotten songs,
Of love that lingers, though time feels wrong.

Yet within sorrow's heavy weight,
Glimmers of hope illuminate fate.
In mourning, grace begins to weave,
Healing threads that we can believe.

So let the tears fall, pure and free,
In this temple, we find unity.
From mourning's depth, the soul takes flight,
In the dawn's embrace, we find the light.

Milton Keynes UK
Ingram Content Group UK Ltd.
UKHW020039271124
451585UK00012B/931